Diplodocus
[DIP-loe-DOE-cus]

Amphicotylus
[am-fee-co-til-us]

Camarasaurus
[camera-sore-us]

Galeamopus
[ga-lay-aa-mo-pus]

Dryosaurus
[dry-o-SORE-us]

T0036086

First published in 2024 by Flying Eye Books Ltd.
27 Westgate Street, London, E8 3RL.

Edited by Sara Forster
Designed by Ivanna Khomyak

1 3 5 7 9 10 8 6 4 2

Published in the US by Flying Eye Books Ltd.
Printed in Poland on FSC® certified paper.

ISBN: 978-1-83874-142-6
www.flyingeyebooks.com

ELLA BAILEY

ONE DAY ON OUR PREHISTORIC PLANET

...WITH A DIPLODOCUS

FLYING EYE BOOKS

As day breaks over an ancient continent,
a young Diplodocus walks among tangled
plants and large trees.

For the first months of her life, she has stayed safe
in the forest, hiding from hungry dinosaurs.

Now she is finally big enough to set out
and search for other Diplodocuses.
They live together in a group called a herd.

She bravely begins her journey across the vast prehistoric plains.

Along the way, she sees many wonderful things . . .

... like a nesting ground littered with countless tiny eggs,

just like the one she hatched from not too long ago.

She passes a group of towering Brachiosaurus who make her feel very small indeed.

While she wanders, she takes time to munch
on her favourite soft leaves and ferns.

Big dinosaurs like her need plenty to eat!

As the day wears on, she pauses for a cool drink under the burning heat of the sun.

In the distance, she hears a strangely familiar sound. Could it be?

GRRRRRR

She marches as quickly as she can towards the rumbling roars . . .

. . . but a hungry Allosaurus finds her first!

An Allosaurus is no match for a Diplodocus.

The little Diplodocus sticks close to the adult's side.

She soon finds lots of friends, some who are just like her . . .

and others who tower over her.

Finally, she has found her new herd.

As night falls, the gentle giants roam across the plains. They eat yummy plants,

sometimes pausing to rest,

or grumble comfortably to one another.

Until the sun rises once more on another day on
our prehistoric planet, a very long time ago.

Apatosaurus
[a-pat-O-sore-us]

Camptosaurus
[camp-to-sore-us]

Gargoyleosaurus
[gar-goil-o-SORE-us]

Torvosaurus
[tore-vo-sore-us]

Nanosaurus
[NAN-oh-SORE-us]